LIFE AND
CHANGING TIMES

The continuing story of Newtownbutler, a border community.

By Barbara Chapman

*An autobiography with some additions by her many friends,
organised by Vicky Herbert.*

Tel: 00 44 (0)28 67721730
email: v.herbert@clonaog.freeserve.co.uk

ISBN - 978-1-907530-16-6

A plan of Newtownbutler after Clarke's House had been demolished to make way for the Crom Road

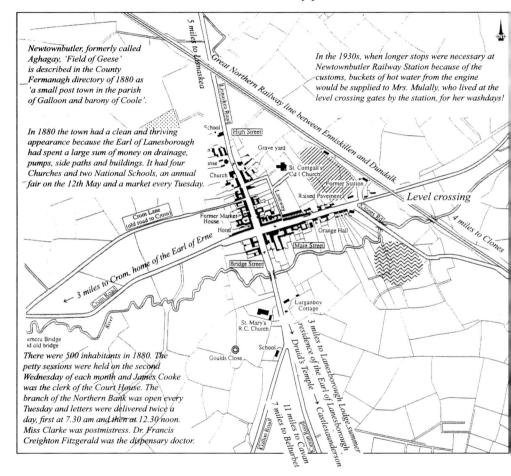

Newtownbutler, formerly called Aghagay, 'Field of Geese' is described in the County Fermanagh directory of 1880 as 'a small post town in the parish of Galloon and barony of Coole'.

In 1880 the town had a clean and thriving appearance because the Earl of Lanesborough had spent a large sum of money on drainage, pumps, side paths and buildings. It had four Churches and two National Schools, an annual fair on the 12th May and a market every Tuesday.

In the 1930s, when longer stops were necessary at Newtownbutler Railway Station because of the customs, buckets of hot water from the engine would be supplied to Mrs. Mulally, who lived at the level crossing gates by the station, for her washdays!

There were 500 inhabitants in 1880. The petty sessions were held on the second Wednesday of each month and James Cooke was the clerk of the Court House. The branch of the Northern Bank was open every Tuesday and letters were delivered twice a day, first at 7.30 am and then at 12.30 noon. Miss Clarke was postmistress. Dr. Francis Creighton Fitzgerald was the dispensary doctor.

Map labels: 5 miles to Lisnaskea; Great Northern Railway line between Enniskillen and Dundalk; Lisnaskea Road; School; High Street; Grave yard; St. Comgall's Cd I Church; Former Station; Level crossing; Church; Raised Pavement; Clones Rd; 4 miles to Clones; Crom Lane (old road to Crom); Former Market House; Laneway; Hotel; Orange Hall; 3 miles to Crom, home of the Earl of Erne; Crom Road; Main Street; Bridge Street; River; umcru Bridge nd old bridge; St. Mary's R.C. Church; School; Goulds Close; Lurganboy Cottage; 3 miles to Lanesborough Lodge, summer residence of the Earl of Lanesborough; Druid's Temple; Castlesaunderson; 11 miles to Cavan; 7 miles to Belturbet

Introduction by Michael McPhillips

When I was asked would I do a short introduction for this book 'Life and Changing Times' of memories of Barbara Chapman, I was delighted to do so. I have lived for over four decades in Bridge Street, Newtownbutler, and many neighbours have come and gone, but Barbara Chapman has been at Lurganboy House all my life. I remember Barbara's father and mother, who have passed to their eternal reward, and remember them as very good neighbours and people who were always there to give support and kindness in times of need to their neighbours, something which Barbara continues right to this day.

I always associated the love of whippet dogs with Barbara and indeed her mother before her, and one in particular, 'Bengy' who Mrs. Chapman often had out for a walk with a little check jacket on it, some thing you didn't see too often in Newtownbutler and a memory of my childhood.

Over twenty years ago I became very good friends with Barbara through our mutual love of local history and we exchanged our knowledge on many occasions at the monthly meeting of our local history society ever since. Local history has no barriers; it belongs to everyone and is a wonderful way to increase one's knowledge of the area and at the same time make friends, sharing a pass-time and enjoying participating. I wish Barbara well with this publication 'Life and Changing Times' and look forward to another one soon again.

Michael McPhillips, Secretary,
Newtownbutler History Society.

Barbara Chapman's dog Daisy
14 years old in 2009

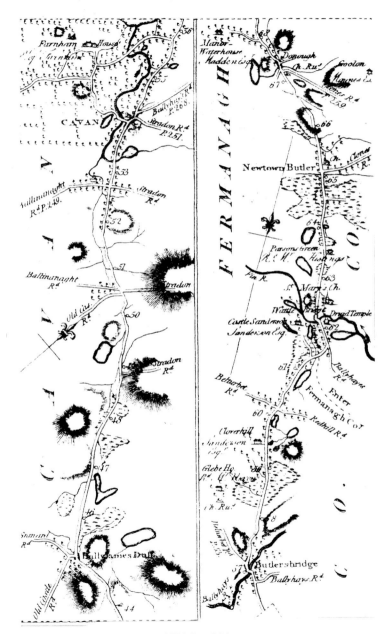

1778 Road Map

2

Index

The Life and Times of Barbara Chapman

Barbara was born in Derbyshire and then her father got a job in Fermanagh as a Customs and Excise Officer. His job was to control the passage of goods across the border, which had been newly formed between Clones and Newtownbutler, but also to distribute pensions. There were Customs Posts at Newtownbutler, Clontivren and Drumboghena.

One of the customs posts, courtesy of Michael McPhillips
The man with the white hat was Mr Lannen, father of Pauline Brown.

When Barbara was a baby her family lived at Forfey just outside Lisnaskea, on the road to the Knocks. They stayed there from 1924 until 1930 when they moved to Newtownbutler. Mrs. Chapman drew water from the well at Curran's house and brought it back to the house on the base of the pram. When Barbara had a bath it was in a tin bath in front of the range. And Mrs. Chapman had an old washing machine which was worked by hand and which Barbara has given to Florencecourt. Most people had an outdoor toilet, and there were chamber pots under the bed. And there was a cesspool at Lurganboy House by the back gate. In fact people didn't get to bathe and wash their hair as much as now, because they had to conserve water. There were always barrels in the garden to catch the rainwater. This was the case with the house at Forfey in 1924 and also at Lurganboy House until the 1960s. There was also a hand-pump for spring water by the house. Mains water came about 1950 or '60. There was a washstand in the bathroom with a cold-water jug and a bowl. The chamber pot was sometimes kept at the bottom of the stand. Oil lamps were used because there was no electricity coming into the house until later.

Barbara's old utensils, lace iron and brass pans

Barbara's rain water tank and pots.

Some more equipment used by Barbara's family. Parrafin oil lamps.

The Maguires of Munville owned the house at Forfey and lent the Chapmans a cow, which Mrs. Chapman milked. There was a fort with a ring of trees there.

Barbara with Anne Curran in front of the Curran house at Forfey

The fort at Forfey where Barbara used to walk

People often forget what it was like years ago, before we had central heating, double-glazing, cavity insulation or even electric blankets. In many cases there was only one fire or range in the house on which everything was done: - cooking the food or heating the water. And there was no hot water until the range or fire was lit. Barbara's family had a small oil stove with two wicks. Often people got dressed in bed because it was too cold to get out of bed to dress.

But life was very simple then, people rode bikes if they had them and the roads were fairly free of traffic. If there were buses, the bus always had a ticket collector or a conductor on it. In some places there were trams, like at Fivemiletown. There were no school buses, since the rural schools were still there to teach children in the small community. This meant less petrol used and also the teachers had more contact with the pupils in a smaller class. Lila Kennedy (nee Whiteman) from Magheraveely used to cycle to the station in Newtownbutler. Because of the difficulty of travelling, there were more children boarding, for example in the Convent, the Collegiate or Portora. Miss Ellis was in charge of boarding at the Collegiate. Children would also take sandwiches for lunch. Education was free up to 14 years of age. Then parents had to pay after that or children left school to work. There were scholarships for a few lucky children. Barbara went to bed at 6.00pm. and her parents usually went to bed at 10.00pm. This saved on light and heating bills. Patchwork quilts were made for the beds out of scraps of material. Some children had to walk for miles to get to school, for example from Galloon to Newtownbutler. Barbara took the train from Newtownbutler into Enniskillen and then walked from the station up to the Collegiate. There was no free transport for pensioners, either! But transport was mostly by donkey and cart or horse and cart in the very old days!

There were hardly any telephones, so contact was maintained by letter writing and visiting. But gramophones (the wind-up kind) and records provided great entertainment, as did the wireless. There were no televisions. Children played games like 'Snakes and Ladders', 'Halma', 'Draughts', 'Chess', 'Ludo', 'Consequences' and they played cards and had pencil and paper games. Outside they played croquet. Barbara went swimming at Derrydoon, there was no swimming pool. But children used row-boats too.

Galloon and the swimming in aid of charity, courtesy of Michael McPhillips

FERMANAGH HERALD *Wednesday 26th June, 2002*

Pictured on the lough shore with well-known local historian and author, John Joe McCusker are Galloon islanders, John McCaffrey (left), Pat Goodwin (2nd right) and Eugene Woods (right).

Galloon residents a happy bunch

There was also a children's newspaper edited by Arthur Mee. It was small in size but very good. There were courts in Newtownbutler and the Knights, the Dolans and the Chapmans used to play tennis and badminton at the Court House. Nowadays there is the internet and computer games are played by all ages! Pocket money can be pretty big now where-as pocket-money was hardly ever heard of in the 1930s and 40s.

Marriage was a lifetime commitment (on the whole) and mothers usually stayed at home with the children, or there was sometimes a nanny to look after the children. There were never any 'latch-key' children like there are nowadays. Sometimes there were maids in the houses who lived in the house where they worked. Even not-so-well-off families could have maids since there were always less fortunate families where a girl needed work of some kind. The maids usually slept in the houses where they worked. Maids sometimes got 30/- a month, and their keep. This meant that there was more home cooking, and more tea parties for the children, and people came to visit more often. Mothers took home cooked food to other older people too. Barbara remembers her mother taking food to a Mrs. Coyle. There was no home help for older people so this was something that was very necessary. The Health Service had yet to start this kind of thing. Homes were real family places, not just to sleep and eat. In fact most babies were born at home, too, not in hospital. The doctors were on call all day from the local surgery. Dr. Fitzgerald had a surgery where Amanda Rickey's shop used to be. Dr. Dolan rebuilt the old manse where the Rev. Sylvers had lived. Nowadays, of course there are benefits for older people, such as home help and the red button to press in emergencies, and exercise machines to help people keep fit.

There used to be a Northern Bank in Newtownbulter but now that branch has closed down and there is only 'The Credit Union'. And there is a street cleaner.

People could go and pick fresh fruit and vegetables at Crom. But also they went picking blackberries in the hedgerows and apples in the orchards. There were no super-markets, just small local shops. There were no deep freezes so food had to be bought in small quantities and kept fresh. Nowadays so much produce is frozen, or imported from abroad. You can shop by email and go to big super-markets, like Asdas.

Of course housework was probably harder. Spring-cleaning was a big job where the carpets and rugs were lifted and taken outside to be beaten. There were no fitted carpets in those days. The coal range had to be cleaned and lit each morning before people could get any hot water or heat. Also the grass was cut with a scythe. Clothes were mostly homemade. (Barbara's mother made most of her own and Barbara's clothes. Barbara still has that sewing machine.)

Barbara, head girl at the Collegiate 1942, taken by W. Hudson, Darling St. Enniskillen.
Barbara's school uniform was made by her mother.

There was a policy of make-do-and-mend, and life had a routine. Sunday was for Church and washing the car. Monday was washday. Tuesday was for the ironing. Wednesday was for mending. Thursday was for gardening, Friday was for shopping and Saturday was for baking, and Saturday night was bath night.

Barbara Chapman's photo of Collegiate ballet, Jill Ritchie, Ann Dickie, Ruth Switzer, Karen Whaley, Linda Rea, Alison Allen, Norma Ritchie

Frances Rea
Margaret Connolly
Jeanette Blair
Detta Kiernan
George Young
Pat Kells (piano)

Barbara's photo Collegiate teachers at Piano

Barbara Chapman with class of pupils at the Collegiate Prep School

Why people will want to be in Courthouse!

Development continues in the village of Newtownbutler with the official launch of a £433,000 project to refurbish its former courthouse building.

The work has been going on since the middle of April, just down the street from the New Faces project which brings adult learning to the doorsteps of local people.

The courthouse projects launch was announced last week by the Newtownbutler Community Development Association. It will also bring a boost to the town when the construction and renovation scheme is complete in December. The former courthouse will provide day care facilities for older people and meeting facilities for local groups like the Thursday Club and the Historical Society.

A large purpose-built hall is also being constructed at the rear of the courthouse where recreational activities such as indoor football, badminton, table tennis and volley ball can take place. The hall is also to be a venue for local dramatic productions.

These facilities are also to be provided as part of the wider Healthy Living Centre Project being developed by the Erne East Partnership, of which the Association is a member. "The idea is to provide a range of services which are directed at well-being, rather than illness," explained Mr. David Lowe, Development Officer for the Upper Erne Link.

The main funder of the project was The EU Special Support programme's Urban Regeneration Fund administered by the DoE, which is giving £330,000 towards the project. The Rural Community Network (Twenty first Century Halls), the Sperrin Lakeland Trust and the Fermanagh District Council are also funders.

Kelly Contracts of Omagh has been appointed to undertake the work under the supervision of Architect Des Ferguson of Arch-Aid Design, Omagh.

At the launch of the community facility project at the old Newtownbutler courthouse are (from left) George Morrisey, Chairman of Belturbet Community Development Association; Tom Crudden, treasurer Newtownbutler Community Development Association; David Lowe, development officer Upper Erne Link; Damien Kelly, Kelly Contracts: Derrick Nixon, Chairman of Fermanagh District Council; Des Ferguson, architect (Arch-Aid Design); Mary Hamilton, Department for Social Development; Helen Gormley, Rural Community Network; Teresa Burns, Sperrin Lakeland Trust; Fergus McQuillan, Chairman of Newtownbutler Community Development Association and Sean Sharkey, committee member.

The beginning of a great community enterprise, with some of Barbara's friends and colleagues. Impartial Reporter 25th May 2000

Barbara, with friends Joyce Herbert and Patsy Bell, with Daisy, her dog. This summer house was originally constructed to help people recover from T.B. when they had to stay outside in the fresh air. During the war the Berkshires and the Seaforth Highlanders played cricket and tennis on the lawn here too.

12

Newtownbutler

All this territory used to belong to the Maguires before the Flight of the Earls in 1607. In fact Eamonn of Coole retired to his stronghold here when he passed over the chieftainship to his son. Newtownbutler was called 'Aghagay' then which meant 'Field of Geese'. Sir Stephen Butler from Belturbet was granted the lands and built a new town here, hence 'Newtownbutler.' One of Sir Stephen's descendents was created Lord Lanesborough and it was after him that 'The Lanesborough Arms' was called.

Some of the best-known places in Newtownbutler were Reilly's Shop and Hotel (Ma Reilly's as the troops knew it, now 'The Lanesborough Arms'), and Bussell's Hotel on the High Street.

Old photo of Main Street, Newtownbutler

Mick Reilly was a tailor and his sister had a 'Holy Shop.' Mrs. Byron sold ice cream in about 1935 in the shop where Lyndon had his butchers shop. It is now a bookies shop. Mr. Brady mended shoes. His shop was near the old railway station.

The railway station and some of the Swindle family travelling to Cork
Photograph courtesy of Linda Swindle.

The Old Railway played a big part in village life. Phil Hueston was signal man. The railway gate and crossing keepers were Johnny McLoughlin, Mr Gribbons and Eddie McAdam. Mr. Lannen was a Land Preventive Man who was connected with the Customs.

Photographs courtesy of Michael McPhillips. Johnny McLoughlin and Mr Chapman on the
right doing his job as Customs & Excise man.

Lifting The Railway at Mc Loughlin's

People coming off the train at Newtownbutler had to have their purchases checked by the customs. April 1923

There were touring plays in the Courthouse, as well as dances, especially during the Second World War. Duffy's circus came to town.

Newtownbutler had a Fair Day, which took place on the street. Cows crossed Barbara's backdoor on their way to the fields. Tommy McManus left fresh (untreated) milk in a can at the back door when he took the cows back to the fields from the milking parlour. The milk wasn't pasteurised but it had lovely cream at the top. Milk came in churns and bottles not in cartons and it had cream on the top. Johnstons owned the farm fields and the land crossed the back door of Lurganboy House. Animals were killed at the Hotel entry.

Michael McPhillips runs a very good Local History group. One of the talks they had was about 'old cures and superstitions.' Another topic was 'The Days of the Railways'. Now Michael is running a series of talks about 'The History of the Famine in the Newtownbutler Area.' It is very well attended with over forty people attending each Thursday session. 'Barbara was always fond of the evenings about local flora and fauna' said Michael.

Paddy O'Rourke making his baskets at the Newtownbutler History Society meeting with Dick Fitzpatrick in the background. Courtesy of Michael McPhillips.

There is also a W.I. Society. Majella Sherry ran an upholstery class.

There were a number of country schools: - Derryginidy, Wattlebridge, Clonmaulin, Gubb Island, Donagh, Ballagh, Drumlone and the Chapel School.

Clonmaulin School

Some of the industry that was around :- Crudden's lace-making, also Mrs. Tierney who lives near Crom now; basket making, also making creels for turf (Johnstons of the Clones Rd. and Malcolm Marshall's maternal grandfather); bringing the turf home; toy making at Crom (Malcolm Marshall); McGilly's on the Crom Road made electricity. James McDonagh's father who lived on Galloon made ash handles for rakes, and was helped by Dick Woods. Farmers made their own hay ropes at the harvest time to tie down the rucks.

Some of the local characters:- Jack Leaghey who organised the firework display, and some well-known families were the Johnstons, the Knights, the Fitzgeralds, the Taylors, the Dolans, the Bells, the Fitzpatricks of Derrydoon, the Lannens, the Moffats.

Some of Barbara's family, friends and colleagues.

Barbara Chapman with Granny Greatorex (DOB 1924, and Barbara's great-grandmother) in Derbyshire.

Barbara Chapman's friend, Anne Loane with her daughter Erica, 1988.

Barbara Chapman is Guiding when it comes to Fermanagh.Last night, a new book which has been her ////////, called "the History of Guiding in Fermanagh", was launched in the Great Hall at Castlecoole where the guest of honour was Lorna Dane the Chief Commissioner.

The 100 page book has been Barbara's 'baby' for the past eight years after she decided it was time to record the history of the movement here.

It was Barbara, a former teacher in Enniskillen Collegiate Prep School and later at the Model Primary School, who held most of the records, but when she realised how enormous the task was going to be she enlisted the help of members of the county committee.

The Guides have been going strong in Fermanagh since the 1920s when the first group was formed and the book traces every step from that day right up to the Ulster Trefoil Guild annual meeting in Garvary just three weeks ago.

It was the Newtownbutler woman who began digging for information from colleagues and former guides, many of which attended the opening last night.

Barbara was guide leader of the 2nd Enniskillen Guides, mainly Collegiate girls, for many years. She was also District Commissioner and Camp Advisor as well as being Chairman of the Trefoil Guild.

She is one of the best known Guiding faces in

FOCUS ON
BOOKS

New book by Barbara Chapman tells the story Guiding in Fermanagh from the very early days

Fermanagh and very much beloved by the guiding movement here.

Sue Hogg, President of the Guides explained that this, to her knowledge, is the first history of guiding in Northern Ireland.

"It is significant in that it pulls together all the historical strands of Guiding in Fermanagh right up to the present day.

"The book covers every single unit of Guides in the county, even if they were only in existence for a short period. It's a significant piece of work and will be appreciated by Fermanagh Guides and former Guides all over the world."

Barbara Chapman enjoying looking over some of her old guide scrap books.

Barbara Chapman with the Chief Guide, Lady Baden-Powell, Freda Carson and Murial Nawn at the Commissioners Conference in Newcastle in 1963.

Presenting the Medal of Merit to Barbara Chapman in 1962. Included are from left, ,Mrs Rogers, Mrs Eadie, Mrs Frith, Lady Langham and Mrs Crozier.

The Duchess of Westminster, a former County Commissioner of the Fermanagh Girl Guides, and Mrs. Warren Loane, the present County Commissioner, greet each other at Castle Archdale on Saturday when the Duchess arrived with the new handbooks to be distributed to the Guides.

FERMANAGH GUIDES

The guides at Crom 1940, photo taken by Barbara herself.

Barbara Chapman and Jean Agnew
as guides

Barbara and Bubbles Knight taken by
the river in Newtownbutler

Bert and Primrose Robinson, Barbara's
good friends and neighbours

Bridget O'Reilly

Freda Allen,
County Commissioner for Guides 2001

Marie McCordick

Barbara's Mother with Ada Malone and Mrs Watts, Easter 1985

Barbara by the stone chair in Newtownbutler,
with the Credit Union and the Hotel in the background.

Mary Woods and her husband lived at Cullion and then moved into the original house at Brown's Bridge (owned by Dr. Dolan who had bought the farm from Mr. Brown.) We used to go there, as children, and enjoyed the old hearth fire and riding the pony. Brown's Bridge was the road to Magheraveely over the GNR railway. Daffodils of various kinds were planted in the bog. They came from Guy Wilson (Co. Antrim). You could get to the bog from the Cavan Road as well as from Dr. Dolan's farm. Dr. Dolan lived at Lurganboy House and then bought the old house, which had been lived in by the Rev. Sylvers (the Methodist Minister). He reconstructed the Manse and lived there for a long time. When he left Lurganboy House it was unoccupied for one and a half years until we came to live there in 1930.

The old maps will show that the level of Lough Erne was much higher before the 1880s. When the water level was dropped by 9 foot it exposed more islands and joined Galloon Island to Gubb. The old road from Newtownbutler to Lisnaskea went from Wattlebridge past Manorwaterhouse.

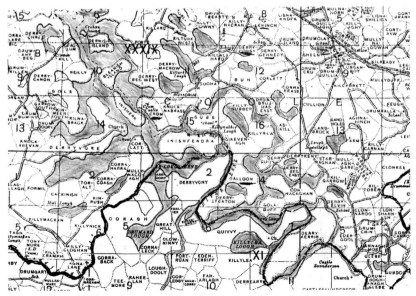

Barbara's father's 1926 map from when he was custom's man

Crom

The name Crom means sloping or crooked and is supposed to refer to the winding of the River Erne in this area.

Prior to 1610 the land was owned by the Maguires, the Chiefs of Fermanagh. Then, under the Plantation scheme of the 17th century, islands and lands were granted to Michael Balfour. He commenced the erection of the castle or fortress in 1611. The building was close to the shore on the south side of the townland of Crom. Michael Balfour came from Fifeshire and brought eight freeholders and lesserholders and four women servants.

Photograph by courtesy of Michael McPhillips. Barge at Crom.

In 1616 Michael Balfour sold the property to Sir Stephen Butler who completed the castle. Early descriptions say that the castle consisted of a 'bawn' 60ft. square with a 22ft lime and stone house within the enclosure.

In 1624 Crom was leased to the Protestant Bishop of Clogher, Dr. James Spottiswood. About the time of the 1641 rebellion it was held by the McManuses. On the death of Dr. Spottiswood in 1644 he bequeathed the castle to his children, one of whom, Mary, married Abraham Creighton in 1655, so the leasehold passed to the Creighton family who had originally come from Edinburgh. It was afterwards converted into perpetuity, subject to a small rent which was bought out by the First Earl of Erne in 1810 from Brinsley, Fourth Earl of Lanesborough, a descendant of the Butler family.

You will note that the early Scottish spelling of Creighton was changed to Crichton at the end of the eighteenth century. The first spelling isn't one that people would recognise now for the Earls of Erne. During the Williamite wars, Crom was of great importance as it commanded the waterway between Belturbet and Enniskillen. Some of the Creighton family distinguished themselves during the two sieges of Crom Castle in 1689.

When Abraham Creighton died he was succeeded by his grandson John who died in 1716 and was buried in Newtownbutler. He was succeeded by his uncle who died in 1728, and then the only surviving son inherited the estate. He was advanced to the peerage of Ireland by the title Baron Erne of Crom in 1768. He died in 1772 and eventually he too was buried in Newtownbutler. The vault can still be seen on the south side of the Church of Ireland in Newtownbutler.

In 1764 when the Creighton family of Crom (later to become the Earls of Erne) were coming home by boat from the housewarming party at Florencecourt they saw a glow in the sky to the South East which told them that their own house at Crom was on fire. It seems this was an accident. Afterwards the family lived mainly in Dublin and when they visited the Crom Estate they probably stayed with Abraham's sister at Knockballymore, near Magheraveely.

The foundation of the new castle was laid in 1831. Edward Blore (an English architect) was commissioned by Colonel John Crichton (note the change of spelling), who later became the Third Earl of Erne, to draw up plans for a castellated Tudor revival mansion, which was completed in 1838.

The Turf House, the Stable Yard and Coach Yard were built about this time and the White Bridge allowed access to the newly built Walled garden on Inisherk Island.

The new castle was burned by fire in 1841. The castle was restored and the new Boat House was built for the use of The Lough Erne Yacht Club.

Near the ruins of the Old Castle are the remains of the 17th Century formal gardens and bowling green enclosed by the Ha-Ha. It also contains the old giant yew trees.

Crichton Tower was built on Gad Island in 1847. Situated near the White Bridge is a Summer House where the family used to take afternoon tea brought by the staff. Below the Summer House are the ruins of the Old Boat House.

Lady Selina Griselda, Countess of Erne and wife of the Third Earl, organised two lace making branches in Fermanagh with the help of normal school teachers in 1852. The school in Lisnaskea was one of the successful ones in the country. The Fourth Earl married Florence Mary Cole who was also interested in lace making but mainly crochet. The lace was made in the homes of workers who lived in poverty. Elizabeth Boyle, the sister of Mary Rogers, historian and wife of the head master of Portora Royal School, wrote a very interesting book on Irish lace making called 'The Irish Flowerers'.

Holy Trinity Church is now the property of the National Trust. It is situated in a picturesque site at the east end of the Derryvore peninsular in the parish of Kinawley and the Diocese of Kilmore. The foundation stone was laid on the 9th June 1840 by John Crichton (afterwards the Third Earl of Erne) and the completed building was consecrated on the 15th July 1842 by the Lord Bishop of the Diocese, John Leslie (D.D.) in the presence of a large congregation. The Church is depicted as a background feature on two paintings entitled 'The Garden Party 1853' and 'Under Sail' c. 1850, both presently at Crom. These show the tower and steeple and the existence of an east window. The porch and old tower were taken down in 1885 to make way for the present tower.

At the west end of the Church, opposite the entrance, is a box-pew reserved for members of the Crichton family. It has seats on two sides and a wooden floor raised 47 cms over the aisle surface to allow for underneath heating.

The red and black tiles were laid down between 1840 and 1847, when the belfry tower was built, but the black painted iron grilles running at intervals down the aisle centre are the originals. These conveyed heat into the Church from a stove located at the west end of the Church under a large grill close to the pew-box. Sometime after 1885 a new heating system was installed, fed from a boiler in the lower basement.

In 1867-9 an arch was cut through the wall at the east end of the nave leading into the chancel which was added at this time, along with a vault and vestry room. These new additions were consecrated by the Lord Bishop of Armagh (M.G. Beresford D.D.) on the 28th September 1869, in memory of Lady Louisa Anne Catherine Crichton, the Earl and Countess of Erne's only daughter, who died at Crom Castle on the 29th August 1866.

There is a very fine east window made by J.B. Capronnier of Brussels, which depicts Christ receiving and blessing the little children. Beneath the window is the inscription 'In Memoriam L.A.C.C. 1886'.

The Church contains many other interesting and historical objects.

The other new addition to the Church built in 1867-9 was the Crichton family vault, which lies underneath the chancel and was entered by lifting a couple of stone slabs outside the east window. These slabs are now covered by turf but apparently rest on steel rails to give accessed below to a door installed by Shirleton of Dundalk. The first person to be buried there was the Lady Louisa Crichton who was interred here in 1868 after an interval of some months from her death, during which time her remains rested in the old family vault at St. Comgall's Church (Newtownbutler) in the Parish of Galloon.

Holy Trinity Church, Courtesy of Michael McPhillips.

Tablets are erected on the wall in memory of Rev. John Thomas Ringwood, Gartside-Tipping and his wife, Jane, the Very Rev. John Maunsell Massy Beresford, Dean of Kilmore and Lt. Commander H.T. Garside Tipping R.N.

There are two large tablets on the west end of the nave, one of these is in memory of John Henry Crichton, Fourth Earl of Erne (1839-1914) and his wife Lady Florence Cole (1849-1924). The other is dedicated to Henry William, Viscount Crichton (1872-1914) and John Henry George Crichton (1907-1940) the father and son who were killed in each of the World Wars.

Incumbents of Holy Trinity Church, and Chaplains to the Earls of Erne were:- Osbert Denton Toosey (1842-3), Archibald Crawford (1843-53), John Haughton Steele (1883-1910). After this date Lord Erne ceased to employ a private chaplain. He entered into an arrangement with the rector of Kinawley Parish. Lord Erne continued to pay all expenses in connection with the Church and its upkeep including the salaries of the sexton, bell-ringer and organist until 1928 when the property and funds were transferred to four trustees.

The following is an extract from the Impartial Reporter of the 18th January 1973:- 'Finally mention should be made of the role the Church played in the life of the people who lived around Upper Lough Erne. The service at Crom Church was 'a rare spectacle' in those early days of the 1900s….some members of the congregation, the farmers and their families came by horse and cart or on foot from the holdings around the lakeshore but the gentry invariably came by boat. At ten minutes to eleven the steamer 'Sirocco' from St. Huberts' and the one from the Cavendish Butler's residence on Inishrath would puff towards the quay below the Church. At the same time the Crom Steamer would round the point of Crom Bay and make her way to join the collection of craft at the quay. Rowing boats brought other worshippers and they all made their way up the winding path to the Church, where the peals of the bell called the faithful.'

In later days a cot was used and a type of floating bridge (chain ferry) was wound across on wires but now a motorboat is used.

The Fourth Earl of Erne died in December 1914 and his son, Viscount Crichton had been killed in October 1914, as mentioned previously, so this left the estate in the hands of trustees between the wars. It was a hard time for everyone concerned because a lot of the men-folk had been killed in the First World War and the 1920s brought the depression, horrendous job shortages and bad harvests. However, Crom Estate kept going with the help of loyal workers.

Inisherk is the island on the far side of the White Bridge. Originally the bridge was made of metal stays and planks of wood similar to railway sleepers. Now this has been replaced by a sturdy construction by which cars and tractors may cross safely to the island. On the island are two cottages and a bothy (overnight accommodation), which were used to house the gardening staff or other members of the retinue serving at the castle.

A Wooton & Sons tractor falling through the old wooden White Bridge
Mrs Chapman, Barbara's mother on left, George Ryan in middle.

Shan Bullock was an author who lived in the cottage near the bridge. He was born in 1865 and died in 1937. His father Thomas, born in 1840, had been the first station- master at Lisnaskea and also a magistrate who was sworn to uphold law and order. Shan's mother was a school teacher and she had eleven children, one of whom died at birth and one was drowned. Growing up on an island was full of interest and he had the companionship of the retainers of the Earl of Erne. His father became Steward of the Crom Estates. Shan wrote 21 books. 'After Sixty Years' and 'The Loughsiders' are of particular interest to those who know Crom but the names he uses are fictitious. The books deal with Ireland's problems both pastoral and social. They are a sincere study of Ulster life of that period.

Mr. Hislop was Head Gardener at Crom from about 1940 and sold fruit and veg from the Walled Garden to local people who could go out and pick strawberries, raspberries or tomatoes. Mr. Hislop also took produce into Wards Shop in Enniskillen. People remember this time with nostalgia and still seem to remember the taste of the strawberries and raspberries! This continued until the 1960s.

The garden had two main paths running at right angles to each other with a lily-pond and palm house at the intersection. There were two beautiful wrought-iron gates at the ends of two of these paths, one of which was made for Lady Davina, the present Earl's mother when she came as a bride to Crom on the 15th July 1931. On both sides of one path were beautiful herbaceous borders. The glasshouses were quite an education for anyone interested in horticulture. Peaches, nectarines and grapes were grown and carefully nurtured. Members of the family were not allowed to pick the fruit themselves because the Head Gardener knew the best to offer them in season.

The bell was hung on one of the trees which was rung at 8.00am to start work and again to announce the lunch break from noon to 1.00pm and again at 6.00pm when work ceased for the day. The potting sheds, packing sheds and the bothy are down this side of the Walled Garden. Kate Moran, the wife of one of the Gardeners and mother to another, Cecil, and Willie, the last Head Gardener, used to live at the end house down this entry-way. Kate's daughter Edna still lives in Lisnaskea.

The Walled Garden and some of the men who worked there.
Isac Faulkner, Cecil and James Moran in front of the strawberries at Crom Estate.

When the fruit and vegetable growing stopped the Walled Garden was used as a venue for rearing pheasants for the shoots, which were held for some years on the estate, but since they have been stopped, it is now used for allotments. There are allotments now at Crom where local people can rent a plot of garden and grow their own produce.

Workers in front of the Walled Garden

Passing the Walled Garden along the path to the lough is a ramp where there was a chain ferry, which took the family and staff to Church, as mentioned before. This cut the journey time to Church since it would have been 16 miles by road. But also there is another quay where the children would wait to be ferried to school. There is a little waiting house built of stone and quite old, but repaired during the war by some of the soldiers based here. That is why we can see corrugated iron in the roof. It was used to shelter the children going to school when the weather was inclement. Sometimes the school cot is moored there, too. The Crom Cot has also been used to take people across to weddings at the Church.

Barbara's photo:- Entrance to the Walled Garden, Crom.

The Summer House, Crom Estate

Bluebells at Old Crom Castle,
courtesy of Clare Ashman

Cot at Crom

to order copies of these please contact greetingscards@businesstypes.co.uk

War-time

The Crichton family had suffered great losses during the wars of the 20th century. Major Henry William Viscount Crichton, son of the Fourth Earl was killed in action in 1914 and the Fifth Earl was killed in action in 1940.

During the Second World War Crom was requisitioned by the War department. The soldiers, who were the Seaforth Highlanders and the Berkshires, were based at Crom and the air-force ground staff was based at Killyroo where William Little lives. American battalions followed these. Nissan huts were erected in the woods of Crom Estate but the officers were billeted in the Castle. Dining huts, wash houses were also erected, and dances were held in the Riding School. Shooting practice was held at the Old Castle and long marches took place all around the area.

Barbara's photo The Old Castle from a boat 2008

Barbara's photo, The Old Castle Crom

Barbara's photo The Boat House Crom

Nowadays the Trust take good care of the Estate and welcome visitors. The Trust organises special events, like cot trips on the lake and open days. The Visitor Centre contact number is 028 677 38118 for enquiries.

The first American troops arrived at Crom on August 28th 1942 and comprised about 750 men from the Tank Destroyer Battalion and they remained until the summer of 1943. The second group of American troops arrived in October or November 1943 and finally left in July or August 1944 to prepare for the setting up of the second front in France. The army finally left Crom and the Castle was derequisitioned on April 4th 1946. Compensation for damage done to the Castle and Estate was paid by the War Department. The Nissan huts were sold to local people. Mr. Corbett, the Estate manager bought most of them as a job lot and sold them off individually afterwards.

During the war there was food-rationing. Rations per person, per week:-bacon, 4 oz; butter, 2 oz; cheese, 2.oz; margarine, 4 oz, milk, 3 pints; cooking fat, 4 oz; sugar, 8 oz; tea, 2 oz; eggs, dried; sweets' 12 oz for 4 weeks. There were meals available on the top floor of the Church Hall in Newtownbutler. The bottom of the Church Hall was an egg-grading place. There were no bananas or oranges in Newtownbutler.

Photograph of American troops as shown in the Visitors Centre, Crom.

Jim Brian said 'Danny and I went to the Railway Bar (in Newtownbutler) and it was run by Maggie McDonagh, an awful nice landlady she was indeed. And we were made most welcome every time that we went in. This particular day was Sunday, as a matter of fact, after the Church parade. We would go down to Maggie's again. So, as you know, it was out of bounds really on a Sunday, at any time to drink there. But anyway, I went in there, enjoying myself with some friends that had come in, and the phone had rung. So she went away and answered the phone. And she came back, and she said, "Well boys," she says, "I think you'd all better go away into the back room and be as quiet as you can. That was the Sergeant on, and that was Belfast after ringing, and they just want to take a wee look around the pubs." So that's where we got in after, and kept quiet until they came round over, and that was it! So it just shows how the co-operation was between the law and the publicans, there.

Another time there was this sergeant, this soldier, had reserves with him, were billeted out and about in the village itself, and the shops were very good at giving them stuff. And this particular shop, it was just as you went down, turned off the main street to go down to Newtownbutler, on the right hand side. This shop was there, and och, it sold everything. However, they were writing home that all the things they could get out, eggs, bacon, butter, you name it, all was there. And, of course, what happened, the letters would get censored, and, of course, everyone was saying to us. So, of course, the law was told, that they would be visiting and going down to take a look at this shop in particular. So, of course they were warned so that they got all the stuff that they shouldn't have had on the ration, and they went out and they hid it in the haystack until everything was law and order. And right enough, when they came, they found nothing. So after that it was "Och no, there never had been stuff there, and never found," and "No, no you don't get that here." They went on about they had just been pulling their friends legs back home as you would say, and making them jealous of all the good things that were happening in Newtownbutler. So there it is that's again how they co-operated with each other.

I remember that before Danny and I went on leave we went down to visit Maggie, down at the Railway Bar, and she had a surprise for us. For we both got a bottle of Hague's Dimple Scotch, you know, those bottles with the three corners, beautifully shaped and you made a lovely light standard out of them. Well, we had that, and we had 200 Gallagher cigarettes each. Well it just shows you what a kind-hearted person Maggie was, and we appreciated it very much indeed. When we got back from our leave, the battalion was already in the process of leaving Newtownbutler. It was actually on the 15th. January that ended our stay there. We were going off to England. Well, we were very sad at leaving Newtownbutler, and we had the memories to go with it.

Some Seaforth Highlanders' memories.

Mr. Chapman, Barbara's father gave up the car because petrol was rationed and people were asked not to travel unless it was extremely necessary.

The troops came often to Newtownbutler to drink, shop and the soldiers arrived or left by the railway, too. This is one of the funny stories told about the troops leaving. Dick Fitzpatrick remembers that the American soldiers had made firm friends with the local people, and especially charmed the children with presents of chewing gum and the ladies with gifts of stockings and Hershy bars. When these troops were due to leave Newtownbutler Station on their way to Europe, many ladies came to say goodbye and wanted to get on the train to see them off at the docks. However, after they had climbed into the second carriage to do so, the Station Master uncoupled that carriage from the first so that when the train chugged out of the Station, the carriage with the ladies in was left behind and only the soldiers left Newtownbutler.

Barabara Chapman's mother and father made sure they were hospitable to the troops and often had soldiers from the Berkshires and the Sea Forth Highlanders to visit. Barbara remembers Sykes Maclean dancing the Scottish Sword Dance in their dinning room and the soldiers playing tennis on the lawn of their house. One American air-force officer sent Barbara a card every Christmas until he died in 2009. His name was W. Lentz, from Baltimore, USA.

During the war windows were taped with sticky tape to save cracks and of course 'black-out restrictions' were in order. No light was to show from houses at night so that the enemy planes would not know. There were air-raid shelters at the Collegiate School.

Newtownbutler Customs and Excise Offices in 1935. Mr Lannen, the L.P.M..

Newtownbutler.   Co. FERMANAGH.

Killowfark House. 2ᴺᵈ June 1904

Local Attractions

Local attractions include Killyfoyle Reservoir which has been turned into a lovely lake to walk round, stocked with fish, Crom Estate, managed by the National Trust, Carn Rock Viewpoint with its Stone Chair, Newtownbutler and Lisnaskea have one too.

Barbara's mum, dad and Dilly at Carnrock

There is also a fine megalithic tomb called 'The Druids Temple' near Wattlebridge on the road to Cavan. From its heights you can see right over the river to Castle Saunderson, another plantation castle. The International Scouts still have ownership of this and hope to soon make it into a centre for scouting activities.

Castle Saunderson which has been bought with a view to transforming it into an international scouting centre.

Reproduced by kind permission of the Impartial Reporter

Stanley Tilson beside one of the standing stones which forms Druid's circle at Wattlebridge. Druid's Temple. Reproduced by kind permission of the Impartial Reporter

Lisnaskea

Again, Lisnaskea was once the capital seat of the Maguire chieftains who were crowned on Cornashee and lived in their stronghold which was where Castle Balfour is now. However, after 1607, Lord Balfour was granted the lands and then in 1822 Lisnaskea, 'Fort of the Whitethorn or Shield' (denoting the crowning ceremonies of the Maguires) was bought by the Third Earl of Erne who then proceeded to build the Market House (the Town Hall where the Northern Bank now stands), the Corn Market and the Butter Market. He also sold the land for the building of Lisnaskea Workhouse which catered for a large catchment area from around the Newtownbutler, Clones, Maguiresbridge and Derrylin area. The nearest Workhouses (some gone now) were in Clones, Bawnboy, Enniskillen, Cavan and Irvinestown (Lowtherstown). There is a great move to restore the Workhouse and use it as a museum and community centre.

The Workhouse

The Corn market

Fennels had a shop where Armstrong's Chemist is now. Harold Fennel was a clergyman and had a sister called Eva.

The stone chair in Lisnaskea

Now there are nursing homes in Lisnaskea called Gortacharn and 'The Fold'. 'The Fold' is actually sheltered accommodation for independent living. Unfortunately, Drumhaw House, next to the Library and a much used residential home in the past has closed.

Some great characters were:- Noel Maguire, John Carron, Pat (the Publican) Cassidy, Dr. Nora Casey, Maurice Watts and many more. The Lisnaskea Historical Society has Pat (the Draper) Cassidy as its president and John Reihill as its Chairman.

Pat (the Draper) Cassidy hard at work. Pat has always been a font of knowledge for everything around Lisnaskea and very helpful to me personally.

John Rehill on his way to Crom.

Old photos and some characters from Barbara's past

The painting class, Lurganboy House c 1950

Guides at Collegiate

Granny Greatorex (1833-1931) with the Duchess of Rutland at the opening of the Rowsley Village Hall

Estelle, Pamela, Jimmy Brady and Barbara

Ernie McSorley and Jimmy Phair 1972

Lurganboy about 1945, on left, Mr. Parry, Aida Malone's father, Mr. & Mrs. Chapman, Ruth Agnew and Kim the dog.

Estelle, Barbara, Pamela and Pam Frizelle.

Barbara at Belturbet Railway.

Barbara with Joyce Herbert in Belleek.

Knockninny

A Mummers centre at Knockninny, based in the old National School, which provides a lot of courses for youngsters about old customs and harvesting is run by Jim Ledwith. There is a 'Holy Well' dedicated to St. Ninniadh near the marina. It is said that its waters cure all kinds of eye ailments. At the marina there is a very nice hotel, which also caters for wedding receptions.

*St. Ninnidh's Well courtesy of
The Impartial Reporter*

Ruins of what is known as 'Knockninny Castle'. Site of Port (Fort) Dobhrain.

*Aughakillymaude Old National School,
1888 - 1988 where the Mummers
Foundation now runs its courses.*

Derrylin

The name of this town, if taken as Doire Fhlainn means the 'oak grove of Flann' or, if taken as Doire Lon, means 'oak grove of the blackbird'. As with ancient names it is hard to tell, but does indicate that originally the land was covered with thick oak woodland. There was a farm belonging to the Augustinians at Callowhill from the 13th and 14th centuries, and it was in the wall of this farm that a carved stone head was discovered and taken to Enniskillen Museum, showing that it was probably the site of a much more ancient culture. The Augustinians were very good at working the land, fertilising properly and reaping the benefits. It was 'reformed' in about 1610 by Bishop Bedell, who founded a church there in the graveyard. The graveyard also holds the tombs of famous Maguire men. The whole area was the original settlement of the Maguire family in Fermanagh, and they alternated living in their strongholds between Knockninny and Lisnaskea.

Callowhill graveyard and ruins of the old 1610 church.

Maguiresbridge

The name of the town dates back to the time the area belonged to the Maguire clan and especially the Tempo Maguires. The bridge across the Colebrook River was built in 1770 by Philip Maguire and you can still see the passing places in the walls of the bridge dating back to when people had to make way for the animal traffic crossing the bridge. The old road from Enniskillen used to cross the river at a ford above the bridge, just by the church. There used to be a great market for butter and eggs and one of the biggest horse fairs in Fermanagh which took place on the Fair Green. These markets were started in 1760 by Brian Maguire and many people can still remember the horse markets, which took place until the mid-1900s.

The Stone Chair in Maguiresbridge sited in the old Fair Green

Tempo

There is a little museum in Tempo run by John McKeagney's family whose excellent book with pictures of all the old places around Fermanagh has been very well received. Unfortunately John died recently and will be missed by everyone who knew him as a real gentleman and friend.

Tempo was the home of the junior branch of the Maguires after the Plantation of Ulster in 1610. They lived at Tempo Manor.

Tempo Manor, owned by the Langhams where Barbara used to take the guides camping.

Some of Johnny McKeagney's drawings.

46